Calm Within

By Ashley Daniel Price

Chapter 1: Introduction to Meditation

Chapter 2: Foundational Techniques

Chapter 3: Advanced Techniques

Chapter 4: Philosophy and Principles of Meditation

Chapter 5: Troubleshooting and Overcoming Challenges

Chapter 6: Deepening Your Practice

Chapter 7: Guided Meditation Scripts

Chapter 8: Meditation and Health

Chapter 9: Mindfulness Meditation

Chapter 10: Different Forms of Meditation

Chapter 11: Meditation and Daily Life

Chapter 12: Conclusion

Appendix: Glossary of Key Terms and Concepts

Chapter 1:

Introduction to Meditation

Welcome to the world of meditation! Meditation is a practice that involves calming the mind, focusing the attention, and cultivating mindfulness. It can help reduce stress, improve mental clarity, enhance emotional well-being, and promote overall relaxation. Get ready to embark on a journey of self-discovery and experience the many benefits of meditation!

As a beginner, it's helpful to know that there are various types of meditation to choose from. Some popular ones include mindfulness, loving-kindness, body scan, and guided meditation. Each type has its unique techniques and focuses, but they all aim to cultivate relaxation, self-awareness, and mental clarity. Exploring different types can help you find what resonates with you and suits your meditation practice.

Mindfulness meditation involves paying non-judgmental attention to the present moment.

Loving-kindness meditation focuses on cultivating compassion and kindness towards oneself and others.

Body scan meditation involves systematically scanning the body for sensations and bringing awareness to each part.

Guided meditation involves following along with a recorded meditation session. These are just a few examples of the diverse range of meditation practices available.

Trying out different types can help you find the one that resonates with you and supports your well-being journey.

To set intentions for your meditation practice, reflect on your purpose, be specific and positive, make it personal, visualize the outcome, and review and renew before each session. Clarify your goals, use clear language, align with your values, visualize success, and stay committed

Chapter 2:

Foundational Techniques

Mindfulness meditation for present-moment awareness

Loving-kindness meditation for cultivating compassion

Body scan meditation for relaxation and body awareness

Breath awareness meditation for calming the mind

To practice mindfulness meditation for present-moment awareness, find a quiet space, sit comfortably, and bring your attention to the present moment without judgment. Observe your thoughts, sensations, and emotions as they arise, and gently bring your focus back to the present moment. Repeat for the duration of your practice.Loving-kindness meditation is a practice that involves cultivating compassion and empathy towards oneself and others. To practice, find a quiet space, sit comfortably, and send well wishes to yourself and others, starting with yourself, loved ones, acquaintances, and even difficult individuals. Repeat with an open and compassionate heart.Body scan meditation involves systematically scanning the body for sensations, bringing relaxation and body awareness. Find a quiet space, lie down or sit comfortably, and bring your attention to each part of the body, noticing sensations without judgment. Repeat, releasing tension and cultivating body awareness.

Breath awareness meditation is a practice that involves focusing on the breath to calm the mind. Find a quiet space, sit comfortably, and bring your attention to the sensation of your breath. Observe each inhale and exhale without judgment, allowing the breath to anchor your awareness and bring calmness to the mind.To choose the best meditation technique for yourself, reflect on your intentions, consider your comfort level, try different techniques, seek guidance if needed, listen to your intuition, and be open to exploration.

Chapter 2:

Foundational Techniques

Choosing the best meditation technique for yourself depends on your individual preferences, needs, and goals. Here are some tips to help you make an informed decision:

Reflect on your intentions: Consider why you want to meditate and what you hope to achieve through your practice. Are you seeking stress reduction, increased mindfulness, emotional regulation, or something else? Understanding your intentions can help guide you towards a meditation technique that aligns with your goals.

Consider your comfort level: Some meditation techniques may require you to sit still for an extended period of time, while others may involve movement or lying down. Reflect on your comfort level and physical capabilities when choosing a meditation technique. It's important to choose a practice that you feel physically comfortable with and can sustain over time.

Try different techniques: Experiment with different meditation techniques to see which ones resonate with you the most. You may find that certain techniques, such as mindfulness meditation, loving-kindness meditation, or body scan meditation, resonate more with your preferences and needs.

Seek guidance if needed: If you're new to meditation, it can be helpful to seek guidance from a qualified meditation teacher, therapist, or mentor. They can provide you with guidance and support in choosing a meditation technique that aligns with your needs and help you develop a consistent practice.

Listen to your intuition: Ultimately, trust your own intuition and inner guidance when choosing a meditation technique. Pay attention to what feels most natural and resonates with you on a personal level. Remember that meditation is a personal practice, and what works best for one person may not work for another.

Be open to exploration: Keep in mind that meditation is a journey of self-exploration and growth. Be open to trying different techniques and be willing to adjust and refine your practice as you progress on your meditation journey.

Remember that the "best" meditation technique is subjective and may vary for each individual. It's important to choose a technique that feels authentic and resonates with your individual needs and preferences. Experiment, reflect, and trust your intuition to find the meditation technique that works best for you.

Chapter 3:

Advanced Techniques

Visualization meditation for enhancing creativity and manifestation
Chakra meditation for balancing energy centers in the body
Mantra meditation for focusing the mind

Walking meditation for integrating mindfulness into daily activities
Visualization meditation is a practice that involves using mental imagery to enhance creativity and manifest desires.
Find a quiet space, sit comfortably, and use your imagination to vividly visualize your desired outcome. Engage all your senses and hold the image in your mind, allowing it to inspire and energize your creative process and manifestation efforts.
Chakra meditation is a practice that involves focusing on the energy centers or "chakras" in the body to balance and align their energy.
 Find a quiet space, sit comfortably, and bring your awareness to each chakra, visualizing their respective colors and qualities, while promoting balance and harmony within your body's energy centers.

Mantra meditation is a practice that involves repeating a word, phrase, or sound ("mantra") to focus the mind and cultivate concentration. Find a quiet space, sit comfortably, and repeat your chosen mantra, such as "Om" or "Peace," with intention and awareness. Allow the repetition of the mantra to help calm the mind and enhance focus.
Walking meditation is a practice that involves bringing mindfulness and awareness to the act of walking, integrating it into daily activities.
Find a peaceful area to walk, and as you walk, pay attention to the sensations in your body, the movement of your feet, and the surrounding environment. Allow walking to become a mindful and meditative experience, bringing presence to each step and moment.
Choosing the best advanced meditation technique for yourself involves reflection, experimentation, seeking guidance if needed, listening to your intuition, and being open to exploration. Trust your inner guidance and choose a technique that resonates with your individual needs and preferences.

Chapter 3:

Advanced Techniques

It's important to remember that meditation is a personal practice, and what may work for one person may not work for another.

It's okay to explore different techniques and find the one that best fits your unique needs and preferences.Reflecting on the journey of meditation and its transformative effects can be a powerful conclusion to your meditation practice. Take a moment to appreciate how meditation has positively impacted your mental, emotional, and physical well-being.Recognize any changes or insights you have gained through your practice, and acknowledge the progress you have made on your meditation journey.

Encouraging readers to continue their meditation practice and integrate it into their lives is crucial for maintaining consistency and reaping the long-term benefits of meditation.

Remind readers that meditation is not a one-time practice, but rather a lifelong journey of self-care and inner exploration.Encourage them to establish a regular meditation routine and make it a part of their daily routine, just like any other healthy habit.Inspiring a lifelong commitment to inner harmony through meditation can be a powerful way to conclude your discussion on the benefits of meditation. Emphasize how meditation is not just a short-term solution, but a lifelong practice that can bring lasting peace, clarity, and well-being.

Encourage readers to cultivate a mindset of self-care and prioritize their mental and emotional health through regular meditation practice, as it can lead to a more harmonious and fulfilling life.

In conclusion, meditation is a powerful practice that offers numerous benefits for the mind, body, and spirit.Through various techniques such as visualization, chakra meditation, mantra meditation, and walking meditation, individuals can cultivate mindfulness, enhance creativity, balance their energy, and focus their minds.

By choosing the right technique for themselves, reflecting on their meditation journey, maintaining consistency, and integrating meditation into their daily lives, individuals can experience the transformative effects of meditation and cultivate a lifelong commitment to inner harmony and well-being.

Chapter 4:

Philosophy and Principles of Meditation

The principles and philosophy behind meditation are rooted in various traditions and belief systems, including Buddhism, Hinduism, Taoism, and mindfulness practices.
These principles often emphasize cultivating mindfulness, awareness, compassion, self-reflection, and non-judgmental observation of thoughts and emotions. Meditation encourages inner exploration, self-awareness, and the development of mental clarity, emotional resilience, and spiritual connection.
The connection between meditation and spirituality lies in the ability of meditation to foster a deeper sense of self-awareness, inner exploration, and connection to something greater than oneself. It can lead to experiences of transcendence, insight, and a deeper understanding of the nature of self, consciousness, and existence, often aligning with one's personal spiritual beliefs and practices.

Delving into different meditation traditions can be a fascinating journey of exploring the rich tapestry of human wisdom and spirituality. From the mindfulness-based practices of Buddhism to the energy-based techniques of Hinduism and the Taoist practices of aligning with the flow of nature, each tradition offers unique approaches to meditation. These approaches may vary in terms of techniques, philosophies, cultural contexts, and intended outcomes. For example, mindfulness practices may emphasize present-moment awareness, compassion, and insight, while mantra meditation may focus on sound and vibration for transcending the mind. Exploring these traditions can provide a deep appreciation for the diversity and richness of meditation as a universal human practice.
Scientific research has increasingly shown the positive effects of meditation on the mind and body. Studies have demonstrated its potential benefits for reducing stress, improving cognitive function, enhancing emotional well-being, promoting physical health, and more. Examining the scientific evidence can provide a deeper understanding of how meditation impacts the brain, physiology, and overall well-being, supporting its integration into modern healthcare and wellness practices.

Furthermore, meditation is not limited to any particular religious or spiritual belief system. It can be practiced by individuals of all backgrounds and faiths, or even those who identify as agnostic or atheist. Meditation is a secular practice that can be approached from a non-religious perspective, focusing solely on the techniques and principles of mindfulness, self-awareness, and mental clarity. This inclusive nature of meditation makes it accessible to people from all walks of life, regardless of their personal beliefs or philosophies.

Philosophy and Principles of Meditation

One of the key aspects of meditation is mindfulness, which involves bringing non-judgmental awareness to the present moment.This practice of observing thoughts and emotions without attachment or judgment allows individuals to develop a deeper understanding of their inner workings and cultivate a sense of self-awareness.Through mindfulness, individuals can learn to respond to their thoughts and emotions in a more skilful and intentional manner, rather than reacting impulsively.This can lead to increased emotional resilience, better decision-making skills, and improved relationships with oneself and others.

Self-reflection is another important aspect of meditation. As individuals practice mindfulness and observe their thoughts and emotions, they are encouraged to reflect on their patterns of thinking, feeling, and behaving. This self-reflective process allows individuals to gain insights into their thought patterns, beliefs, and behaviors, and to develop a deeper understanding of themselves.Self-reflection can lead to personal growth, self-improvement, and a greater sense of self-compassion and acceptance.Compassion is another central theme in many meditation practices. Through cultivating compassion towards oneself and others, individuals can develop a kinder and more compassionate attitude towards themselves and the world around them.

Compassion meditation often involves sending positive intentions, love, and goodwill towards oneself, loved ones, acquaintances, and even towards those who may be perceived as difficult or challenging. This practice of extending compassion towards oneself and others can foster a greater sense of connectedness, empathy, and kindness, contributing to a more harmonious and compassionate world.In addition to these philosophical principles, meditation also has physical benefits. Research has shown that regular meditation practice can have a positive impact on physical health, including reducing stress, lowering blood pressure, improving sleep quality, and boosting the immune system. Meditation has also been shown to have positive effects on cognitive function, such as improving focus, attention, and cognitive flexibility. These physical and cognitive benefits further support the integration of meditation into modern healthcare and wellness practices.

In conclusion, meditation is a practice that is rooted in various traditions and belief systems, with principles that emphasize mindfulness, self-awareness, compassion, self-reflection, and non-judgmental observation. It is a secular practice that can be practiced by individuals of all backgrounds and faiths, and its benefits have been supported by scientific research. Meditation offers not only physical and cognitive benefits but also has the potential to foster deeper self-awareness, personal growth, and spiritual connection. Exploring different meditation traditions and incorporating meditation into one's daily routine can lead to a more mindful, compassionate, and fulfilling life.

Chapter 5:

Troubleshooting and Overcoming Challenges

Meditation practice can come with its own set of challenges and obstacles, such as difficulty with focus, restlessness, racing thoughts, and lack of consistency. Addressing these challenges may involve developing patience, self-compassion, and resilience, and implementing strategies like guided meditation, mindfulness techniques, creating a conducive environment, and establishing a consistent routine. Understanding and addressing these common obstacles can support a more fulfilling and sustainable meditation practice.

Practical tips for dealing with distractions, restlessness, and doubts:

- Acknowledge distractions without judgment and gently bring your focus back to the meditation object.
- Use grounding techniques, such as deep breathing or body scan, to calm restlessness.
- Practice self-compassion and non-judgment towards doubts or thoughts that arise during meditation.
- Experiment with different meditation techniques or styles to find what resonates with you.
- Create a conducive environment for meditation, free from unnecessary distractions.
- Set realistic expectations and be patient with yourself as you develop your meditation practice.
- Seek guidance from experienced practitioners or meditation teachers for personalized tips and support.

Troubleshooting physical discomfort and dealing with emotions during meditation:

- Adjust your posture to ensure comfort and alignment of the body.
- Use props, such as cushions or blankets, to support your body during meditation.
- Notice and observe physical discomfort or emotions without judgment or attachment.
- Use mindfulness techniques, such as labeling or nothing, to acknowledge and let go of emotions or physical sensations.
- Practice self-care, such as gentle stretching or relaxation techniques, before and after meditation to ease physical discomfort.
- Seek guidance from a qualified meditation teacher or healthcare professional for specific physical or emotional concerns during meditation.
- Remember that emotions and physical sensations are natural during meditation and can be part of the healing and transformative process.

Chapter 5:

Troubleshooting and Overcoming Challenges

Overcoming resistance and maintaining consistency in meditation practice:
Maintaining consistency in meditation practice can be challenging, as resistance may arise due to various factors, such as busy schedules, distractions, and doubts. Here are some tips for overcoming resistance and maintaining consistency:

- **Reflect on your motivation:** Take some time to reflect on the reasons why you started meditation in the first place and the benefits you hope to gain from it. Keeping your motivation in mind can help you stay committed to your practice.
- **Set realistic goals:** Set achievable and realistic goals for your meditation practice, considering your schedule and other commitments. It's better to start with shorter sessions that you can easily fit into your routine, rather than aiming for long sessions that may be difficult to sustain.
- **Create a consistent routine:** Establish a regular meditation routine that works for you, whether it's daily, a few times a week, or whatever frequency you can manage. Consistency is key in building a sustainable meditation practice.
- **Cultivate self-discipline:** Develop self-discipline by setting clear intentions, creating a dedicated meditation space, and minimizing distractions during your practice. Remember that meditation is a skill that requires regular practice to improve.
- **Use accountability strategies:** Hold yourself accountable by using accountability strategies, such as keeping a meditation journal, setting reminders, or finding a meditation buddy who can provide support and encouragement.
- **Practice self-compassion:** Be gentle with yourself if you miss a session or encounter challenges in your practice. Practice self-compassion and forgiveness, and avoid self-judgment or guilt, which can hinder your motivation.
- **Experiment with different techniques:** Explore different meditation techniques or styles to find what resonates with you. Trying out different techniques can help you stay engaged and motivated in your practice.

Celebrate progress: Acknowledge and celebrate the progress you make in your meditation practice, no matter how small. Recognize the positive changes and benefits you experience, which can reinforce your motivation to continue.

Remember that building a consistent meditation practice takes time and effort. Be patient with yourself, stay committed to your practice, and be open to adjusting your approach as needed. With persistence and self-compassion, you can overcome resistance and maintain a consistent and fulfilling meditation practice.

Chapter 5:

Troubleshooting and Overcoming Challenges

Meditation can be a powerful tool to tackle problems and overcome challenges due to its numerous benefits for the mind and body. Here are some key reasons why meditation is a valuable approach for troubleshooting and overcoming challenges:

- Stress reduction: Challenges can often trigger stress, which can impact our mental and physical well-being. Meditation has been shown to reduce stress by activating the relaxation response in the body, helping us manage stress more effectively and approach challenges with a calmer mindset.
- Emotional regulation: Challenges can bring about a range of emotions, and meditation can help us regulate our emotions by developing emotional intelligence and self-awareness. Through mindfulness and self-compassion practices, we learn to observe and acknowledge our emotions without judgment, allowing us to approach challenges with a more balanced emotional state.
- Improved cognitive function: Meditation has been shown to improve cognitive function by enhancing attention, concentration, and cognitive flexibility. This can sharpen our cognitive abilities, enabling us to approach challenges with improved mental acuity and problem-solving skills.
- Enhanced creativity and intuition: Meditation allows for the free flow of ideas and insights by quieting the mind and creating a space of mental clarity. This can help enhance our creativity and intuition, aiding in finding unique and effective solutions to challenges.
- Increased self-awareness: Meditation encourages self-awareness, which allows us to identify patterns, triggers, and biases that may be contributing to the challenges we are facing. By gaining insight into our own thoughts, emotions, and behaviors, we can make conscious choices to address challenges in a more effective manner.
- Cultivation of patience and acceptance: Meditation can help cultivate patience and acceptance, as it teaches us to be present with the current moment without constantly striving for a different outcome. This allows us to approach challenges with a more patient and equanimous mindset, which can be beneficial in navigating through difficult situations.
- Greater resilience: Meditation fosters qualities such as resilience, perseverance, and adaptability, which can help us bounce back from challenges and setbacks with greater strength and determination.

In summary, meditation is a valuable approach to tackle problems and overcome challenges due to its ability to reduce stress, regulate emotions, improve cognitive function, enhance creativity and intuition, increase self-awareness, cultivate patience and acceptance, and foster resilience. Incorporating meditation into our daily routine can help us develop a more mindful and resilient mindset, enabling us to approach challenges with greater clarity, calmness, and effectiveness.

Chapter 6:

Deepening Your Practice

Deepening your meditation practice involves going beyond the surface level and exploring the depths of your inner experience. It may involve further refining your technique, increasing your meditation time, incorporating advanced practices, and cultivating a deeper understanding of yourself, your mind, and your emotions.

Exploring advanced techniques for experienced meditators may involve delving into more intricate and specialized meditation practices that require a higher level of focus, concentration, and awareness. These techniques may include advanced forms of breathwork, visualization, concentration, insight, or transcendental meditation, among others. They can provide deeper insights, expanded states of consciousness, and profound spiritual experiences for those who have a solid foundation in meditation and are seeking to further deepen their practice.

Cultivating a meditative mindset in daily life involves integrating mindfulness, presence, and awareness into your everyday activities. It means bringing the qualities of calmness, clarity, and non-judgmental awareness to your interactions, tasks, and experiences throughout the day. It involves living with conscious intention, being fully present in the moment, and applying the principles of meditation to your thoughts, emotions, and actions in your daily life.

Incorporating meditation into different aspects of life, such as relationships, work, and self-care:Incorporating meditation into different aspects of life involves recognizing that meditation is not limited to a formal practice on a cushion or mat, but can also be integrated into various areas of our lives. For example, in relationships, meditation can help cultivate patience, empathy, and compassionate communication. In work, meditation can enhance focus, creativity, and productivity. In self-care, meditation can aid in managing stress, improving sleep, and promoting overall well-being. It involves applying the principles of meditation, such as mindfulness, self-awareness, and non-judgment, to different situations and contexts, allowing us to bring a meditative mindset and skilful awareness to all aspects of our lives.Expanding awareness and mindfulness beyond formal meditation sessions:Expanding awareness and mindfulness beyond formal meditation sessions involves extending the practice of mindfulness and conscious awareness to our daily activities, interactions, and experiences. It means being fully present, attentive, and non-judgmental in each moment, whether it's during routine tasks, conversations, or leisure activities. It involves cultivating a continuous state of mindfulness and integrating it into our lives, so that it becomes a natural and effortless way of being, rather than just a practice reserved for formal meditation sessions.

Chapter 6:

Deepening Your Practice

Deepening your practice with any type of meditation involves committing to a regular practice and exploring ways to enhance your experience. Here are some ways to deepen your meditation practice:

- Consistency: Regularity is key to deepening your meditation practice. Set aside a specific time and place for meditation, and aim to practice consistently, whether it's daily, weekly, or on a schedule that works best for you. Consistent practice helps to train your mind and create a habit of meditation, allowing you to go deeper in your practice over time.
- Longer sessions: Consider gradually increasing the duration of your meditation sessions. Starting with shorter sessions and gradually extending them can help you build mental stamina and allow for deeper states of relaxation and focus.
- Mindful awareness: Pay attention to the quality of your meditation practice, focusing on being fully present in the moment without judgment. Cultivate a state of mindful awareness by observing your breath, bodily sensations, thoughts, and emotions as they arise without getting attached to them. This can help you develop a deeper level of self-awareness and insight.
- Deep breathing: Incorporate deep, slow breaths into your meditation practice. Deep breathing can help activate the relaxation response in the body, promoting a deeper sense of relaxation and calmness during meditation.
- Concentration techniques: Experiment with different concentration techniques, such as focusing on a specific object, repeating a mantra, or visualizing. These techniques can help you develop greater focus and concentration, allowing for a deeper experience of meditation.
- Body scan: Include a body scan practice in your meditation routine. This involves systematically scanning your body from head to toe, paying attention to sensations and releasing any tension or discomfort. This can help you develop a deeper connection with your body and cultivate a sense of relaxation and awareness.
- Guided meditation: Consider using guided meditation sessions to deepen your practice. Guided meditations can provide guidance and structure, helping you to go deeper into a meditative state and explore different aspects of your mind and consciousness

Deepening Your Practice

The benefits of deepening your meditation practice are numerous. Deepening your practice can lead to a greater sense of relaxation, calmness, and mental clarity. It can help you develop improved focus, concentration, and self-awareness. Deepening your practice can also promote emotional well-being, resilience, and insight into your thoughts, emotions, and behaviors. Regular and deep meditation practice has been associated with various physical, mental, and emotional health benefits, including reduced stress, improved cognitive function, enhanced emotional regulation, increased mindfulness, and overall well-being.

In summary, deepening your meditation practice involves consistency, mindful awareness, concentration techniques, body scan, and utilizing guided meditation, among other techniques. Regular and deep meditation practice can lead to a range of benefits for your mind and body, supporting your overall well-being and personal growth.

Chapter 7:

Guided Meditation Scripts

Guided meditation scripts are written or spoken instructions that guide individuals through a meditation practice. They provide a structured framework for meditation, helping practitioners focus their attention, relax their body, calm their mind, and cultivate specific qualities or states of mind, such as mindfulness, relaxation, self-compassion, or visualization. Guided meditation scripts can be used in various settings, including group meditation sessions, meditation apps, online resources, or personal practice, to guide individuals through different types of meditation and facilitate their meditation experience.Collection of guided meditation scripts for various purposes,including stress reduction, self-compassion, gratitude, and relaxation:

A collection of guided meditation scripts can be a valuable resource for individuals looking to incorporate meditation into their daily routine. These scripts provide step-by-step instructions that guide practitioners through a meditation practice for various purposes, such as stress reduction, self-compassion, gratitude, relaxation, and more.For instance, a guided meditation script for stress reduction may include techniques such as deep breathing, body scan, and visualization to help individuals relax their body and calm their mind. It may also incorporate mindfulness techniques to increase awareness of the present moment and cultivate a non-judgmental attitude towards thoughts and emotions.

Similarly, a guided meditation script for self-compassion may include affirmations, imagery, and compassionate language to cultivate kindness, acceptance, and self-care towards oneself. It may also involve acknowledging and validating one's emotions and experiences with a gentle and compassionate approach.

A guided meditation script for gratitude may involve guiding individuals to focus their attention on positive aspects of their life and express appreciation for them. It may also encourage individuals to cultivate a mindset of gratitude and appreciation towards oneself, others, and the world around them.Guided meditation scripts for relaxation may include techniques such as progressive muscle relaxation, visualization of calming scenes, and guided imagery to help individuals relax their body, calm their mind, and release tension or stress.These scripts can be used in various settings, such as group meditation sessions, meditation apps, online resources, or personal practice, to guide individuals through a meditation practice and facilitate their experience. They can be adapted or customized to suit individual preferences, needs, and levels of experience with meditation.

Overall, a collection of guided meditation scripts can provide individuals with a variety of options to choose from based on their specific needs, interests, and goals in their meditation practice. They can serve as a helpful tool in enhancing relaxation, reducing stress, cultivating self-compassion, and promoting overall well-being.

Chapter 7:

Guided Meditation

ScriptsStep-by-step instructions for practicing guided meditations:Practicing guided meditations can be a helpful way to incorporate meditation into your daily routine. Here are step-by-step instructions for practicing guided meditations:

- Find a quiet and comfortable space: Choose a location where you won't be disturbed and can sit or lie down comfortably. You may use a meditation cushion, chair, or lie down on a yoga mat or blanket.
- Choose a guided meditation: Select a guided meditation script or recording that aligns with your intentions or goals for meditation, such as stress reduction, self-compassion, or relaxation. You can find guided meditations online, through meditation apps, or in books/resources.
- Set your intention: Take a moment to set your intention for the meditation. What do you hope to cultivate or achieve through this practice? This could be relaxation, mindfulness, self-compassion, or any other specific goal you have in mind.
- Follow the guidance: Press play or read through the guided meditation script, and allow yourself to follow along with the instructions. The guide may lead you through breathing exercises, body scans, visualizations, or other techniques to help you relax and focus your mind.
- Stay present: As you listen to the guided meditation, try to stay present and attentive to the sensations in your body, your breath, and the guidance provided. If your mind wanders, gently bring it back to the present moment without judgment.
- Cultivate mindfulness: Use guided meditation as an opportunity to cultivate mindfulness, which involves paying attention to the present moment with an attitude of curiosity, openness, and non-judgment. Be aware of your thoughts, emotions, and sensations without trying to change or control them.
- Practice self-care: Be gentle with yourself and practice self-care during the guided meditation. If any discomfort arises, whether physical or emotional, acknowledge it with compassion and allow yourself to experience it without judgment or resistance.
- End with gratitude: As the guided meditation comes to an end, take a moment to express gratitude for yourself, the practice, and any insights or experiences you had during the meditation.
- Reflect and integrate: After the guided meditation, take a few moments to reflect on your experience and how it may impact your daily life. Consider ways to integrate mindfulness or other insights from the practice into your daily activities and interactions.Remember that guided meditations are just one form of meditation practice, and you can also explore other meditation techniques to find what works best for you. Regular practice and patience are key to cultivating a meaningful meditation practice.

Chapter 7:

Guided Meditation Scripts

Tips for creating your own personalized guided meditation scripts:

Creating your own personalized guided meditation scripts can be a fulfilling and effective way to customize your meditation practice to your unique needs and intentions. Here are some tips for creating your own guided meditation scripts:

- **Set your intention:** Start by clarifying your intention or goal for the meditation. What do you want to focus on or cultivate? It could be relaxation, stress reduction, self-compassion, gratitude, or any other specific intention that resonates with you.
- **Choose a structure:** Decide on the structure or format of your guided meditation script. Will it include breathing exercises, body scans, visualizations, or other techniques? Consider the length of the meditation and how you want to guide the practitioner through the practice.
- **Use clear and simple language:** Write your guided meditation script using clear and simple language. Avoid jargon or complex terms that may be confusing to the practitioner. Use descriptive and sensory language to create vivid and engaging imagery.
- **Incorporate mindfulness and self-care:** Infuse your guided meditation script with mindfulness and self-care elements. Encourage the practitioner to be present in the moment, to notice their thoughts, emotions, and sensations with non-judgmental awareness, and to practice self-compassion and self-care throughout the meditation.
- **Be mindful of pacing and tone:** Consider the pacing and tone of your guided meditation script. Use a calm and soothing tone of voice, and allow for pauses to give the practitioner time to fully experience each step of the meditation. Avoid rushing or overwhelming the practitioner with too much information or guidance.
- **Tailor to individual preferences:** Keep in mind that everyone has different preferences, so try to create a guided meditation script that resonates with a wide range of practitioners. Avoid making assumptions or using language that may exclude or alienate certain individuals.
- **Test and refine:** Once you've created your guided meditation script, test it by practicing it yourself or with a small group. Pay attention to how it feels, if it flows well, and if it effectively meets your intended goal. Refine and revise your script as needed based on feedback and your own observations.
- **Practice with authenticity:** Lastly, remember to practice with authenticity and genuine presence when guiding others in meditation. Let your own experience and voice shine through, and connect with the heartfelt intention behind your guided meditation script.

Creating your own personalized guided meditation scripts can be a creative and empowering way to tailor your meditation practice to your individual needs and preferences. Experiment with different techniques, styles, and themes to create a guided meditation that resonates with you and supports your well-being.

Chapter 8:

Meditation and Health

Research has shown that meditation can have a positive impact on both physical and mental health. Some of the health benefits of meditation include:

Reducing stress and anxiety: Meditation can help to lower the levels of the stress hormone cortisol in the body, which in turn can help to reduce feelings of stress and anxiety.

Improving sleep: Regular meditation has been shown to improve sleep quality and duration, which can help to improve overall health and wellbeing.

Lowering blood pressure: Studies have shown that regular meditation can help to lower blood pressure, which can reduce the risk of heart disease and stroke.

Boosting immune function: Meditation has been shown to boost immune function by increasing the production of antibodies and improving the body's ability to fight off infections.

Reducing symptoms of depression: Research has shown that meditation can be an effective tool for reducing symptoms of depression and improving overall mood.

Managing chronic pain: Studies have shown that meditation can help to reduce the severity of chronic pain, and may be particularly effective for conditions such as fibromyalgia and lower back pain.

Improving cognitive function: Regular meditation has been shown to improve cognitive function, including memory, attention, and decision-making meditation and Health

Meditation has been practiced for thousands of years and is often associated with Eastern traditions such as Buddhism and Hinduism. However, in recent years, it has become increasingly popular in the Western world as a tool for improving physical and mental health.

Research has shown that regular meditation practice can have a range of health benefits. For example, studies have found that it can help to reduce stress and anxiety by lowering levels of the stress hormone cortisol in the body. This can have a positive impact on a wide range of health outcomes, as chronic stress has been linked to a range of physical and mental health problems, including heart disease, diabetes, and depression.

Meditation has also been shown to improve sleep quality and duration, which can have a significant impact on overall health and wellbeing. Poor sleep has been linked to a range of negative health outcomes, including an increased risk of obesity, diabetes, and heart disease.

In addition to its mental health benefits, meditation has been shown to have positive effects on physical health. For example, it can help to lower blood pressure, reduce symptoms of chronic pain, and boost immune function. These benefits are thought to be due to the relaxation response that occurs during meditation, which can help to reduce inflammation in the body and improve overall physiological functioning.

Overall, the evidence suggests that meditation can be a powerful tool for improving both physical and mental health. It is a simple practice that can be incorporated into daily life, and has the potential to have a significant impact on overall health and wellbeing.

Chapter 9:

Mindfulness Meditation

Mindfulness meditation is a powerful tool that can benefit your mind, body, and spirit in countless ways. It involves paying attention to the present moment, without judgment or distraction, which can help you feel more grounded and centered.

One of the key benefits of mindfulness meditation is that it can reduce stress and anxiety. By focusing on the present moment, you can let go of worries about the past or future, which can help you feel more relaxed and at ease. This, in turn, can lower your cortisol levels and reduce inflammation in the body, which are both associated with chronic stress.

In addition, mindfulness meditation can also improve your mental clarity and focus. By training your mind to stay focused on the present moment, you can improve your ability to concentrate and stay on task, which can be especially helpful for those who struggle with distractions or attention deficit disorders.

Mindfulness meditation can also have physical benefits, such as reducing pain and improving sleep quality. By focusing on your body and breath, you can become more aware of physical sensations and learn to release tension and discomfort. This can be especially helpful for those with chronic pain conditions or sleep disorders.

Moreover, mindfulness meditation can enhance your emotional well-being by increasing feelings of compassion and empathy towards yourself and others. By cultivating a non-judgmental attitude towards your thoughts and feelings, you can become more accepting and kind towards yourself, which can help you develop a more positive outlook on life.

Finally, mindfulness meditation can help you connect with your spiritual side by allowing you to become more attuned to your inner self. By tuning into your intuition and inner wisdom, you can develop a deeper sense of purpose and meaning in your life, which can be transformative for your overall sense of well-being.

Here are some additional benefits of mindfulness meditation:

Improved Relationships: Practicing mindfulness can help improve relationships by developing a greater sense of empathy and compassion towards others. When we are mindful, we become more attuned to our own thoughts and feelings, which can help us better understand the thoughts and feelings of others. This can lead to more harmonious relationships and better communication.

Better Decision Making: When we practice mindfulness, we learn to observe our thoughts and emotions without getting carried away by them. This helps us make better decisions by giving us more clarity and insight into our own minds. We become less reactive and more responsive to situations, allowing us to make more thoughtful and considered choices.

Reduced Symptoms of Depression: Mindfulness meditation can be an effective tool for managing symptoms of depression. By increasing awareness of our thoughts and emotions, we can develop a greater sense of control over our mental state. This can lead to a reduction in symptoms of depression, such as negative self-talk, rumination, and feelings of hopelessness.

Increased Resilience: Practicing mindfulness can help us become more resilient to stress and adversity. By training ourselves to observe our thoughts and emotions without judgment, we can develop a greater sense of equanimity and calmness, even in difficult situations. This can help us bounce back from setbacks and challenges more easily.

Improved Physical Health: Mindfulness meditation has been shown to have a range of physical health benefits. It can lower blood pressure, reduce inflammation in the body, and boost the immune system. It can also improve sleep quality and reduce the risk of chronic diseases, such as heart disease and diabetes.

Greater Creativity: Mindfulness can help boost creativity by allowing us to access new ideas and perspectives. When we are mindful, we become more aware of our surroundings and can notice things that we might not have noticed before. This can help us generate new ideas and insights, leading to greater creativity.

Greater Sense of Well-Being: Mindfulness meditation can help us develop a greater sense of well-being by helping us connect with our inner selves. When we are mindful, we become more aware of our thoughts, emotions, and physical sensations, which can help us develop a deeper sense of self-awareness and self-acceptance. This can lead to greater happiness, fulfillment, and overall well-being.

Overall, mindfulness meditation is a powerful tool that can benefit us in countless ways. Whether we are looking to reduce stress, improve our relationships, boost our creativity, or simply feel more connected to ourselves and the world around us, mindfulness can help us achieve our goals. By making mindfulness a regular part of our daily routine, we can cultivate greater awareness, clarity, and inner peace, leading to a happier, healthier, and more fulfilling life.

Chapter 10:

Different Forms of Meditation

There are many different forms of meditation, each with its own unique focus and techniques. Here are some of the most common forms of meditation:

Mindfulness Meditation: Mindfulness meditation involves paying attention to the present moment, without judgment or distraction. The focus is on being aware of your thoughts, feelings, and physical sensations, and observing them without getting caught up in them. The goal is to develop greater self-awareness and acceptance, leading to greater peace and well-being.

Transcendental Meditation: Transcendental Meditation is a technique that involves silently repeating a mantra, which is a word or phrase that is believed to have a calming effect on the mind. The goal is to achieve a deep state of relaxation and inner peace, which can help reduce stress and anxiety.

Loving-Kindness Meditation: Loving-kindness meditation involves cultivating feelings of love, kindness, and compassion towards oneself and others. The focus is on sending positive energy and goodwill to others, which can help reduce negative emotions such as anger and resentment.

Body Scan Meditation: Body scan meditation involves focusing on the physical sensations in your body, one part at a time. The goal is to develop greater awareness of your body and to release tension and stress.

Zen Meditation: Zen meditation is a form of meditation that originated in Japan. It involves focusing on your breath and observing your thoughts without getting caught up in them. The goal is to achieve a state of deep calm and inner peace.

Vipassana Meditation: Vipassana meditation is a form of meditation that originated in India. It involves focusing on your breath and observing your thoughts and physical sensations without judgment. The goal is to develop greater awareness and insight into the nature of reality.

Yoga Meditation: Yoga meditation involves practicing yoga poses and breathing exercises, with the goal of achieving greater physical and mental balance. The focus is on developing strength, flexibility, and inner peace.

Chakra Meditation: Chakra meditation is a form of meditation that focuses on the seven energy centers in the body, known as chakras. The goal is to balance these energy centers and promote greater physical and emotional health.

Mantra Meditation: Mantra meditation involves silently repeating a word or phrase that is believed to have spiritual significance. The goal is to achieve a state of inner peace and transcendence.

In summary, there are many different forms of meditation, each with its own unique techniques and focus. From mindfulness meditation to chakra meditation to yoga meditation, each form of meditation can help promote greater physical, mental, and emotional health. Whether you are looking to reduce stress, improve your relationships, or achieve a greater sense of inner peace and well-being, there is a form of meditation that can help you achieve your goals.

Chapter 11:

Meditation and Daily Life

Meditation is an ancient practice that has been used for thousands of years to promote physical, mental, and spiritual well-being. It is a technique that involves focusing the mind on a particular object, thought, or activity to increase awareness and achieve a state of inner calm and relaxation. In today's fast-paced world, stress and anxiety are common problems that can have a significant impact on our health and happiness. Incorporating meditation into your daily routine can help reduce stress and anxiety, improve sleep quality, boost immune function, and reduce symptoms of depression.

There are many different types of meditation, each with its own unique benefits and techniques. Here are some of the most popular types of meditation:

Mindfulness Meditation

Mindfulness meditation involves focusing on the present moment without judgment. The goal is to become aware of your thoughts and feelings without getting caught up in them. Mindfulness meditation can help reduce stress and anxiety, improve sleep quality, and promote a greater sense of well-being.

To practice mindfulness meditation, find a quiet place where you can sit comfortably. Focus your attention on your breath, noticing the sensation of the air as it enters and leaves your body. When your mind wanders, simply bring it back to your breath without judgment.

Transcendental Meditation

Transcendental meditation is a technique that involves the use of a mantra or sound to help quiet the mind. The goal is to achieve a state of deep relaxation and inner peace. Transcendental meditation has been shown to reduce stress and anxiety, improve cognitive function, and promote a sense of well-being.

To practice transcendental meditation, find a quiet place where you can sit comfortably. Close your eyes and repeat a mantra or sound silently to yourself. Allow your mind to become calm and quiet, focusing on the sound of the mantra.

Loving-Kindness Meditation

Loving-kindness meditation involves cultivating feelings of love and kindness towards oneself and others. The goal is to promote a sense of compassion and connectedness with the world around you. Loving-kindness meditation has been shown to reduce stress and anxiety, improve mood, and promote social connection.

To practice loving-kindness meditation, find a quiet place where you can sit comfortably. Begin by focusing on yourself and silently repeat the phrases "may I be happy, may I be healthy, may I be at peace." Then, focus on someone you care about and repeat the phrases "may they be happy, may they be healthy, may they be at peace." Continue this practice, expanding your circle of compassion to include all living beings.

Yoga Meditation

Yoga meditation is a practice that combines physical movement with breath work and meditation. The goal is to achieve a state of balance and harmony between the body, mind, and spirit. Yoga meditation has been shown to improve flexibility, reduce stress and anxiety, and promote overall health and well-being.

To practice yoga meditation, find a quiet place where you can practice yoga poses comfortably. Focus on your breath as you move through the poses, allowing your mind to become calm and quiet.

Choosing the Best Type of Meditation for You?

The key to choosing the best type of meditation for you is to experiment with different techniques and see what works best for your needs and lifestyle. You may want to try out a few different types of meditation and see which ones resonate with you the most. You can also consult with a meditation teacher or attend a meditation class to get guidance and support.

Incorporating Meditation into Daily Life

Once you have found a type of meditation that works for you, it's important to incorporate it into your daily life. This may involve setting aside a specific time each day to meditate, such as first thing in the morning or before bed. It may also involve finding ways to integrate mindfulness into your daily activities

For example, you can practice mindfulness while you're brushing your teeth, walking to work, or eating a meal.

One of the benefits of incorporating meditation into your daily routine is that it can help you develop greater self-awareness and emotional regulation. When you meditate regularly, you become more attuned to your thoughts, feelings, and bodily sensations. This can help you identify patterns of thought and behavior that may be causing you stress or anxiety. With this increased awareness, you can then take steps to address these patterns and cultivate a greater sense of calm and well-being.

Another benefit of incorporating meditation into your daily routine is that it can help you manage stress more effectively. When you meditate, you activate your body's relaxation response, which helps counteract the effects of the stress response. This can help reduce symptoms of anxiety, such as increased heart rate and rapid breathing. In addition, regular meditation practice has been shown to lower levels of the stress hormone cortisol, which can help improve overall health and well-being.

Meditation can also help improve sleep quality. When you meditate before bed, you can help calm your mind and reduce racing thoughts that can interfere with sleep. In addition, regular meditation practice has been shown to help reduce symptoms of insomnia and improve overall sleep quality.

One of the challenges of incorporating meditation into daily life is finding the time and motivation to practice regularly. To overcome this challenge, it can be helpful to set a specific time each day for meditation and make it a non-negotiable part of your routine. You can also find ways to make meditation more enjoyable and engaging, such as listening to soothing music, using aromatherapy, or practicing in a group setting.

In summary, incorporating meditation into daily life can have many benefits for physical, mental, and spiritual well-being. It can help reduce stress and anxiety, improve sleep quality, boost immune function, and promote a greater sense of well-being. To choose the best type of meditation for you, it's important to experiment with different techniques and see what works best for your needs and lifestyle. Once you have found a technique that resonates with you, it's important to make it a non-negotiable part of your daily routine. With regular practice, you can cultivate greater self-awareness, emotional regulation, and overall health and well-being.

Chapter 12:

Conclusion

Reflecting on the journey of meditation and its transformative effects, one can witness the profound changes that occur within oneself over time. From increased self-awareness and emotional regulation to improved focus and creativity, meditation offers a path of self-discovery and personal growth.

As you continue your meditation practice, remember that consistency and patience are key. The effects of meditation may not always be immediate or linear, but with regular practice, you can cultivate a deeper connection with yourself, others, and the world around you. Integrating meditation into your daily life can bring a sense of peace, balance, and mindfulness to your activities, relationships, and work.

I encourage you to stay committed to your meditation practice, even when faced with challenges or distractions. Remember that meditation is a skill that can be developed over time, and progress may come in waves. Embrace the journey, and be kind to yourself as you navigate your meditation practice.

As you continue on your meditation path, I hope you are inspired to make meditation a lifelong commitment to inner harmony. Embrace the ongoing practice of meditation as a way to nourish and support your physical, mental, emotional, and spiritual well-being. May it become an integral part of your daily routine, guiding you towards greater self-awareness, mindfulness, and personal growth.

In conclusion, meditation is a truly transformative practice that offers a myriad of benefits for our overall well-being. Reflect on the positive effects it has on your life, stay committed to your practice, and integrate it into your daily routine. Let meditation be a lifelong journey towards inner harmony, self-awareness, and personal growth. Embrace the profound and lasting effects of meditation, and may it continue to enrich your life in countless ways.

Meditation is a powerful practice that has been rooted in various traditions and belief systems for centuries, and its benefits are supported by both ancient wisdom and modern scientific research. Whether you choose mindfulness meditation, mantra meditation, loving-kindness meditation, or any other type of meditation, dedicating just 10 or 15 minutes a day to this practice can have a profound impact on your overall health, mind, and soul.

Meditation provides a multitude of benefits for the mind, body, and spirit. It can reduce stress, improve cognitive function, enhance emotional well-being, promote physical health, and foster self-awareness and personal growth. Through cultivating mindfulness, awareness, compassion, and non-judgmental observation, meditation encourages inner exploration, mental clarity, emotional resilience, and spiritual connection. It can lead to experiences of transcendence, insight, and a deeper understanding of the self, consciousness, and existence.In today's fast-paced world, where stress, anxiety, and distractions are prevalent, taking the time to meditate can be a valuable tool for self-care and self-nourishment. Meditation provides an opportunity to pause, connect with oneself, and tap into the inner resources for healing, growth, and transformation. It allows for a deeper sense of relaxation, calmness, and clarity in the mind, which can positively impact various aspects of life, including work, relationships, and overall well-being. Moreover, meditation is a practice that can be customized to suit individual preferences, beliefs, and lifestyles. It is accessible to people of all ages, backgrounds, and abilities. You don't need any special equipment or expertise to start meditating. Just a quiet space, a comfortable posture, and a willingness to be present in the moment are enough to begin your meditation journey.Incorporating meditation into your daily routine can be a small but powerful step towards improving your overall health, mind, and soul. Just dedicating a few minutes a day to this practice can help you cultivate a greater sense of peace, clarity, and self-awareness. As with any new habit, consistency is key, and with regular practice, you may start to experience the positive effects of meditation in your life. In conclusion, meditation is a time-tested practice that offers a myriad of benefits for the mind, body, and soul. Spending just 10 or 15 minutes a day in meditation can contribute to improved well-being, enhanced self-awareness, and a deeper connection with oneself and the world. Consider incorporating meditation into your daily routine and experience the transformative effects it can have on your overall health and well-being.

Appendix

Glossary of Key Terms and Concepts

- **Meditation:** A practice of focusing the mind and achieving a heightened state of awareness and relaxation for various purposes, such as improving mental clarity, reducing stress, and cultivating mindfulness.
- **Mindfulness:** The quality of being fully present and aware of the present moment without judgment. Mindfulness is often cultivated through meditation and can be applied to everyday activities for increased awareness and engagement.
- **Concentration:** The ability to focus the mind on a single object or point of attention, such as the breath or a mantra, as a way to quiet the mind and achieve a meditative state.
- **Breath awareness:** A type of meditation that involves focusing on the breath as the object of concentration. It is a common form of meditation used for calming the mind and developing mindfulness.
- **Body scan:** A form of meditation that involves systematically scanning and bringing awareness to different parts of the body, often used for relaxation, stress reduction, and body awareness.
- **Loving-kindness meditation:** A type of meditation that involves cultivating feelings of love, compassion, and kindness towards oneself and others, often used to develop empathy, compassion, and positive emotions.
- **Visualization:** A form of meditation that involves using the mind's eye to create mental images or scenes, often used for enhancing creativity, manifestation, and relaxation.
- **Mantra:** A word, phrase, or sound that is repeated during meditation to help focus the mind and achieve a meditative state. Mantra meditation is often used for developing concentration and calming the mind.
- **Chakras:** Energy centers in the body, according to some Eastern spiritual traditions, which are believed to influence physical, mental, and emotional well-being. Chakra meditation involves focusing on these energy centers for balancing and aligning the body's energy.
- **Guided meditation:** A form of meditation that involves following along with a recorded or live meditation session led by a meditation teacher or guide, often using verbal cues and instructions to facilitate the meditation experience.
- **Self-compassion:** The practice of being kind, understanding, and accepting towards oneself, often cultivated through meditation and used for developing self-care, self-love, and self-acceptance.
- **Inner harmony:** A state of balance, peace, and alignment within oneself, often cultivated through regular meditation practice and used for promoting overall well-being, self-awareness, and personal growth.

I hope this glossary provides you with a helpful overview of key terms and concepts related to meditation. Remember that different traditions and practices may have unique interpretations and variations of these terms, and it's important to explore and find what resonates with you in your meditation practice.